My United States

Iowa

ANN O. SQUIRE

Children's Press®
An Imprint of Scholastic Inc.

Content Consultant

James Wolfinger, PhD, Associate Dean and Professor
College of Education, DePaul University, Chicago, Illinois

Library of Congress Cataloging-in-Publication Data
Title: Iowa / by Ann O. Squire.
Description: New York, NY : Children's Press, an imprint of Scholastic Inc., 2018. | Series: A true book | Includes
   bibliographical references and index.
Identifiers: LCCN 2017051375 | ISBN 9780531235591 (library binding) | ISBN 9780531250785 (pbk.)
Subjects: LCSH: Iowa—Juvenile literature.
Classification: LCC F621.3 .S64 2018 | DDC 977.7—dc23
LC record available at https://lccn.loc.gov/2017051375

Photographs ©: cover: Tim Thompson/Getty Images; back cover bottom: Eddie Brady/Getty Images; back cover ribbon: AliceLiddelle/
Getty Images; 3 bottom: Radharc Images/Alamy Images; 3 map: Jim McMahon/Mapman ®; 4 left: atoss/iStockphoto; 4 right: Paul
Starosta/Getty Images; 5 top: Michael Rolands/iStockphoto; 5 bottom: All Canada Photos/Alamy Images; 7 center top: Zack Frank/
Shutterstock; 7 bottom: The Hawk Eye, Melissa Jansson/AP Images; 7 center bottom: David Howells/Corbis/Getty Images; 7 top:
Gina Kelly/Alamy Images; 8-9: MaxyM/Shutterstock; 11: Philip Scalia/Alamy Images; 12: Alex Maclean/Getty Images; 13 background:
PickStock/iStockphoto; 13 inset: David Greedy/Stringer/Getty Images; 14: Clint Farlinger/Alamy Images; 15: Kevin E. Schmidt/
ZUMAPRESS.com/Alamy Images; 16-17: Monte Goodyk/Getty Images; 19: MICHAEL B. THOMAS/AFP/Getty Images; 20: Tigatelu/
Dreamstime; 22 right: grebeshkovmaxim/Shutterstock; 22 left: BigAlBaloo/Shutterstock; 23 bottom right: All Canada Photos/Alamy
Images; 23 top left: Paul Starosta/Getty Images; 23 center: DNY59/iStockphoto; 23 top right: johnyoo7pan/iStockphoto; 23 bottom
left: Madlen/Shutterstock; 24-25: Daniel Eskridge/Stocktrek Images/Science Source; 27: A. Zeno Shindler/The Granger Collection; 29:
Ed Vebell/Getty Images; 30 top left: North Wind Picture Archives/Alamy Images; 30 bottom: MPI/Stringer/Getty Images; 30 top right:
Council Bluffs Ferry and a Group of Cottonwood Trees, Iowa, 1853 (w/c on paper), Piercy, Frederick (fl.1848-82)/Museum of Fine Arts,
Boston, Massachusetts, USA/Gift of Maxim Karolik for the M. and M. Karolik/Bridgeman Images; 30 bottom: Railroad Bridge over the Des
Moines River 1900 (photo)/Universal History Archive/UIG/Bridgeman Images; 31 top right: Matt McClain/ The Washington Post/Getty
Images; 31 top left: BigAlBaloo/Shutterstock; 32: Scott Olson/Getty Images; 33: Universal History Archive/UIG/Getty Images; 34-35:
Michael Rolands/iStockphoto; 36: Telegraph Herald, Jessica Reilly/AP Images; 37: America/Alamy Images; 38: Timothy Fadek/Corbis/
Getty Images; 39: f11photo/Shutterstock; 40 inset: bhofack2/iStockphoto; 40 background: PepitoPhotos/Getty Images; 41: Andy Abeyta,
Quad-City Times/ZUMA Wire/Alamy Images; 42 top right: DEA PICTURE LIBRARY/Getty Images; 42 center right: Stock Montage/Getty
Images; 42 bottom left: Bettmann/Getty Images; 42 bottom right: Michael Ochs Archives/Getty Images; 42 top left: Everett Collection
Inc/Alamy Images; 43 top left: Silver Screen Collection/Getty Images; 43 top center: Michael Mauney/The LIFE Images Collection/Getty
Images; 43 top right: Moviestore collection Ltd/Alamy Images; 43 center: Susuan Wood/Getty Images; 43 bottom center: JSC/NASA; 43
bottom right: Gregg DeGuire/WireImage/Getty Images; 43 bottom left: Everett Collection Historical/Alamy Images; 44 top right:
dcwcreations/Shutterstock; 44 top left: Gary Fandel/Bloomberg/Getty Images; 44 bottom left: atoss/iStockphoto; 44 bottom right:
OLEKSANDR PEREPELYTSIA/iStockphoto; 45 top left: rruntsch/iStockphoto; 45 top right: axnjax/iStockphoto; 45 bottom: MaxyM/
Shutterstock.

Maps by Map Hero, Inc.

All rights reserved. Published in 2019 by Children's Press, an imprint of Scholastic Inc.
Printed in North Mankato, MN, USA 113

SCHOLASTIC, CHILDREN'S PRESS, A TRUE BOOK™, and associated logos are trademarks and/or registered trademarks of Scholastic Inc.

Scholastic Inc., 557 Broadway, New York, NY 10012

1 2 3 4 5 6 7 8 9 10 R 28 27 26 25 24 23 22 21 20 19

Front cover: Des Moines

**Back cover: Iowa Advanced
Technology Laboratories**

Welcome to Iowa

Find the Truth!

Everything you are about to read is true *except* for one of the sentences on this page.

Which one is **TRUE**?

T or F Much of Iowa's tallgrass prairie has been destroyed and replaced by farmland.

T or F Iowa is one of our nation's most densely populated states.

Find the answers in this book.

Contents

THE BIG TRUTH!

Wild prairie rose

What Represents Iowa?

Corn

4

Hot-air balloons

Eastern
goldfinch

This Is Iowa!

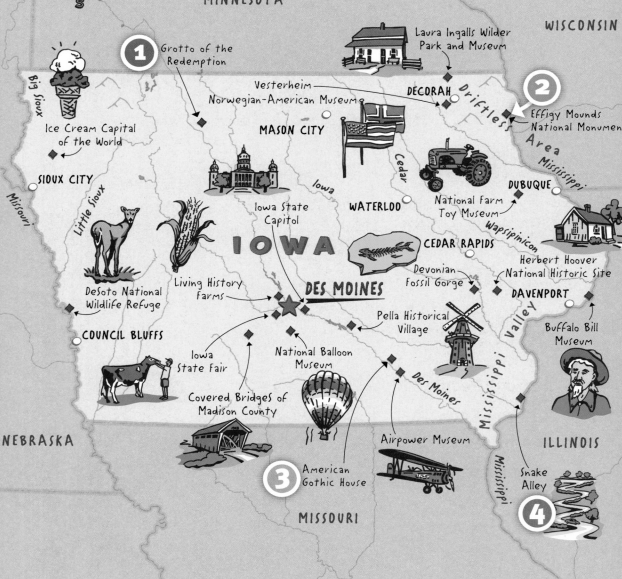

MINNESOTA

WISCONSIN

① Grotto of the Redemption

Laura Ingalls Wilder Park and Museum

② Effigy Mounds National Monument

Driftless Area

Big Sioux

Vesterheim Norwegian-American Museum

DECORAH

Ice Cream Capital of the World

MASON CITY

Mississippi

National Farm Toy Museum

DUBUQUE

SIOUX CITY

Missouri

Little Sioux

Iowa

Cedar

WATERLOO

Wapsipinicon

Herbert Hoover National Historic Site

IOWA

Iowa State Capitol

CEDAR RAPIDS

Devonian Fossil Gorge

DAVENPORT

DeSoto National Wildlife Refuge

Living History Farms

DES MOINES

Pella Historical Village

Buffalo Bill Museum

COUNCIL BLUFFS

Iowa State Fair

National Balloon Museum

Mississippi Valley

Covered Bridges of Madison County

Des Moines

Airpower Museum

Snake Alley

ILLINOIS

③ American Gothic House

Mississippi

④

NEBRASKA

MISSOURI

0   40
Miles

1 Grotto of the Redemption

This religious shrine is a huge, ornate structure covering one block in the city of West Bend. The walls and ceilings are encrusted with shells, gems, and semiprecious stones. The Grotto was the life's work of German-American priest Paul Dobberstein.

2 Effigy Mounds National Monument

These earthen mounds in the shapes of birds, bears, and other animals were constructed approximately 1,000 years ago by Native Americans.

3 American Gothic House

One of the most famous paintings in American art is *American Gothic* (1930) by artist Grant Wood. It shows two people in front of a farmhouse. The house that inspired the painting is in the city of Eldon.

OHIO

4 Snake Alley

"The Crookedest Street in the World," Snake Alley, is in the city of Burlington. Faced with a hill that was too steep for a straight road, city planners designed the street with a series of sharp turns.

Iowa has 30.6 million acres
(12.4 million hectares)
of farmland.

CHAPTER 1

Land and Wildlife

Located in the midwestern region of the United States, Iowa covers 55,857 square miles (144,669 square kilometers) of land area, making it the country's 23rd-largest state. Although it's a big state, Iowa is not densely populated. With just over three million people living in Iowa, the state ranks 30th in population.

Surrounded by States

Iowa borders six states: South Dakota to the northwest, Minnesota to the north, Wisconsin to the northeast, Illinois to the east, Missouri to the south, and Nebraska to the west. Major rivers flow along Iowa's eastern and western boundaries. To the east is the Mississippi River, and to the west are the Missouri and Big Sioux Rivers.

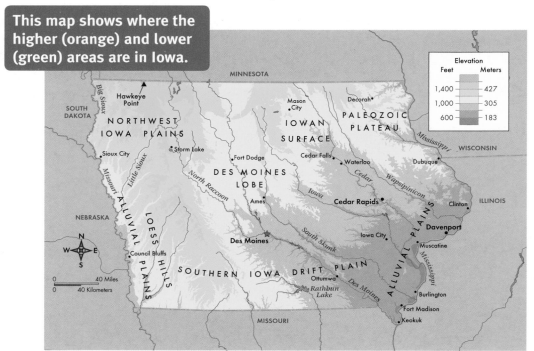

This map shows where the higher (orange) and lower (green) areas are in Iowa.

A worker moves spools of thread used to weave cloth at the Amana Colonies.

The Amana Colonies

The Amana **Colonies** are a group of seven villages founded by German immigrants in the 1800s. Early residents of the now historic site kept to themselves and only interacted with outsiders to buy or sell goods. They established farms and grew all their own food. They also made their own clothing, furniture, and other goods. By the 1880s, the population of the Amana Colonies had grown to more than 1,800 people. Visitors today can get a good sense of this area's German heritage.

Highs and Lows

Iowa's **terrain** consists mainly of flat plains and gently rolling hills. The **elevation** doesn't change very much throughout the state. Iowa's lowest point is 480 feet (146 meters) above sea level. It is in the southeast, where the Des Moines River meets the Mississippi River. Its highest spot is Hawkeye Point in northwestern Iowa. This peak measures 1,670 feet (509 m) in elevation.

Flowing about 2,350 miles (3,782 kilometers), the Mississippi River is the second-longest river in the country.

MAXIMUM
TEMPERATURE
118°F

MINIMUM
TEMPERATURE
-47°F

Iowa's floods can cause damage to homes and make travel difficult.

Though plants need water to grow, too much water at once can kill crops.

Hot, Cold, and Everything in Between

In Iowa, summers can be hot, sticky, and humid, while winter temperatures drop well below freezing. Springtime often brings thunderstorms, which may be accompanied by hail, high winds, and even tornadoes. If a hailstorm occurs when crops are growing, it can do a lot of damage. Flooding (from too much rain) and droughts (from too little rain) can also affect crops. But even with these extremes, Iowa's **climate** is well suited for **agriculture**.

13

Vegetation

Before the land was cleared for farming, much of Iowa was covered with tallgrass **prairie**. As the name suggests, the major plants in this **ecosystem** were tall grasses. These provided **habitats** for many types of animals, including many different mammals, birds, reptiles, and butterflies. Dense forests and wetlands covered other parts of the state. Over the years, most of those habitats were destroyed, and today over 85 percent of Iowa's land has been converted to farmland.

Rolling Thunder Prairie State Preserve protects 123 acres (50 ha) of Iowa's remaining prairie ecosystem.

Bison can still be seen today in natural areas such as the Neal Smith National Wildlife Refuge.

Iowa's Wildlife

The conversion of Iowa's natural ecosystems to farmland has had a big impact on the state's wildlife. In the 1800s, bison, lynx, mountain lions, wolves, and minks could be found throughout the state. So could a wide variety of birds, fish, and reptiles. But as the woodlands, prairies, and wetlands have changed, many of these species have become rare or even disappeared completely from the state.

Iowa's state capitol is the only one in the country with five domes.

CHAPTER 2

Government

Iowa's first capital was Iowa City, a town in the eastern part of the **territory**. After Iowa became a state in 1846, it was decided that the capital should be closer to the center of the state. This would make travel easier for lawmakers. Des Moines was chosen in 1857, and the new capitol was completed in 1886. Iowa's grand state capitol stands atop a hill, offering visitors a wide view of the city.

Three Branches

Iowa's state government is made up of three branches. The executive branch is headed by the governor. It carries out laws and is responsible for the state's many departments and agencies. Iowa's legislative branch consists of the Senate and the House of Representatives. Members propose new laws and vote on whether to pass them. The judicial branch is made up of the court system.

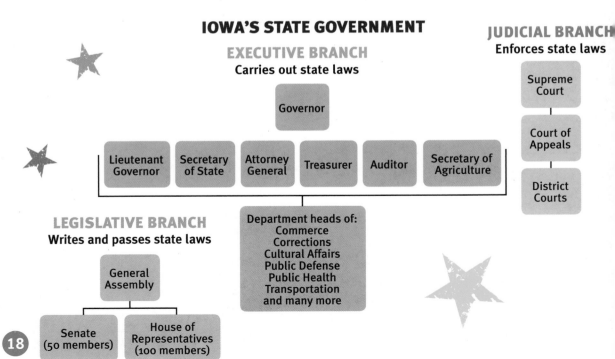

IOWA'S STATE GOVERNMENT

EXECUTIVE BRANCH
Carries out state laws

Governor

Lieutenant Governor | Secretary of State | Attorney General | Treasurer | Auditor | Secretary of Agriculture

Department heads of:
Commerce
Corrections
Cultural Affairs
Public Defense
Public Health
Transportation
and many more

JUDICIAL BRANCH
Enforces state laws

Supreme Court

Court of Appeals

District Courts

LEGISLATIVE BRANCH
Writes and passes state laws

General Assembly

Senate (50 members) | House of Representatives (100 members)

Voters participate in the 2016 Iowa caucus event in Keokuk. Caucuses are usually held at fire departments, schools, and other public places throughout the state.

The Iowa Caucus

Every four years, Iowa kicks off the nationwide presidential campaign by holding the Iowa **caucus**. During the caucus, members of the country's major political parties vote on which candidate should represent their party in their general presidential election. Each state holds a similar event, but Iowa is always the first. This means the results get a lot of media attention. They can also have a big effect on the overall presidential campaign. For example, Barack Obama won the Iowa caucus in 2008 and went on to win the presidency.

Iowa in the National Government

Each state elects officials to represent it in the U.S. Congress. Like every state, Iowa has two senators. The U.S. House of Representatives relies on a state's population to determine its numbers. Iowa has four representatives in the House.

Every four years, states vote on the next U.S. president. Each state is granted a number of electoral votes based on its number of members in Congress. With two senators and four representatives, Iowa has six electoral votes.

2 senators and 4 representatives

6 electoral votes

With six electoral votes, Iowa's voice in presidential elections is below average compared to other states.

The People of Iowa

Elected officials in Iowa represent a population with a range of interests, lifestyles, and backgrounds.

Ethnicity (2016 estimates)

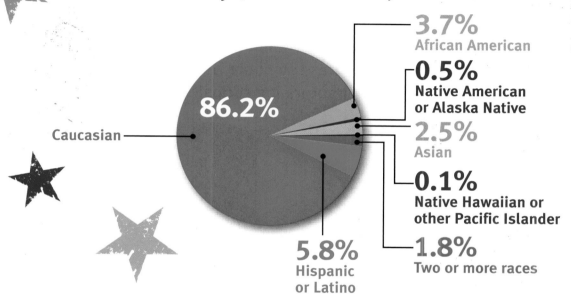

86.2% Caucasian

3.7% African American

0.5% Native American or Alaska Native

2.5% Asian

0.1% Native Hawaiian or other Pacific Islander

1.8% Two or more races

5.8% Hispanic or Latino

More than **1/4** of the population have a college degree.

7.5% of Iowa residents speak a language other than English at home.

11.8% of Iowans are living below the poverty level.

16.4% of the population are over 65 years old and

23.3% are under 18 years old.

91.7% of the population graduated from high school.

71.1% of Iowans own their homes.

THE **BIG** TRUTH!

What Represents Iowa?

States choose specific animals, plants, and objects to represent the values and characteristics of the land and its people. Find out why these symbols were chosen to represent Iowa or discover surprising curiosities about them.

Seal

The state seal was created in 1847, one year after Iowa became a state. It shows a soldier standing in a field of wheat. Around him are symbols important to Iowa's history: farming, mining, transportation, and the Mississippi River. An eagle holds a banner with the state motto: "Our liberties we prize and our rights we will maintain."

Flag

The blue stripe on the state flag stands for loyalty and truth. The white stripe stands for purity, and the red one stands for courage. The design and colors of the flag are similar to the flag of France. This reflects Iowa's history as part of the French Louisiana Territory.

Wild Prairie Rose

STATE FLOWER

This pink rose is found throughout Iowa and blooms from June through late summer.

Geode

STATE ROCK

Geodes have a hard outer shell and a lining of sparkling quartz crystals. Southeastern Iowa is the best place in the state to find them.

Oak

STATE TREE

This tree offers shelter, food, and nesting space for many kinds of animals in Iowa.

Tama Soil

STATE SOIL

This deep, rich soil is one of the most productive types for use in agriculture.

Eastern Goldfinch

STATE BIRD

The male goldfinch is bright yellow and black, while the female is a dull brownish yellow.

The last mammoths died out sometime around 1650 BCE.

CHAPTER 3

History

Humans first came to the land that is now Iowa about 11,500 years ago, after **glaciers** from the last Ice Age had receded. The terrain was very different then. Forests covered the land, and the climate was cooler and wetter than it is now. Early peoples survived by hunting large mammals such as mammoths, mastodons, and giant bison. As time went on, the landscape changed. Prairies became more common, and people began to hunt smaller mammals such as deer and elk.

Native Iowans

As years passed, Iowa's Native Americans began to create permanent settlements. The Woodland culture emerged in about 500 BCE. Woodland people lived in round homes made from wood, mud, and straw. They farmed corn and a variety of grains. The Woodland people also built huge earthen mounds in the shapes of animals. Many of the mounds still exist today.

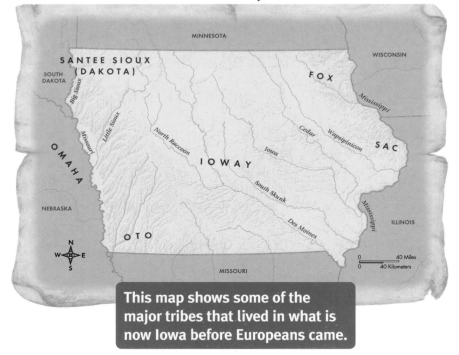

This map shows some of the major tribes that lived in what is now Iowa before Europeans came.

New Arrivals

By the 1600s, many different groups lived in Iowa and western Illinois, including the Sac and the Fox. In 1673, explorers Jacques Marquette and Louis Jolliet became the first Europeans to visit Iowa. Several years later, another explorer claimed all

Chief Moses Keokuk (left) led the Sac and Fox Nation during the mid- to late 1800s.

of present-day Iowa for France. But France didn't do much with the land, and in 1803 it sold the huge Louisiana Territory to the United States for $15 million. Eventually, all or part of 15 states, including Iowa, were created out of that land.

The Lewis and Clark Expedition

After buying the Louisiana Territory, President Thomas Jefferson decided that America should know more about its new land. He sent Meriwether Lewis and William Clark to explore the area. The expedition took more than two years. On the way, Lewis and Clark met many Native Americans, mapped much of the new land, and encountered plants and animals they had never seen before.

This map shows routes Europeans took as they explored and settled what is now Iowa.

Battle of Bad Axe, Black Hawk War, 1832

Effigy Mounds

Wisconsin

Mississippi

Big Sioux

Little Sioux

Missouri

North Raccoon

Cedar

Wapsipinicon

Iowa

South Skunk

Platte

Des Moines

Mississippi

N W E S

Louis Jolliet and Father Jacques Marquette, 1673		Stephen H. Long, 1819–1820		0 40 Miles
Father Louis Hennepin, 1680		Mound		0 40 Kilometers
Lewis & Clark, 1804–1806		Battle		
		Present-day state of Iowa		

Lewis and Clark began their journey by traveling along the Missouri River in a boat.

Westward Expansion

The United States began to expand westward, which forced Native Americans out of their homelands. In 1832, they resisted the government's attempts to push them out of the area, but they were eventually defeated. They were forced to give up a 50-mile-wide (80 km) strip of land in eastern Iowa along with land in Illinois. Most of Iowa's first white settlers came to this area, which was known as the Black Hawk Purchase.

Settling the Prairie

Most newcomers came from Pennsylvania, New York, Ohio, and other states. They were used to trees and forests, so the vast prairies of the Midwest came as a shock. Instead of using timber to build houses, many used sod (the top few inches of soil, held together by grass and roots). Instead of burning wood for fuel, they used dried animal droppings, hay, and corncobs.

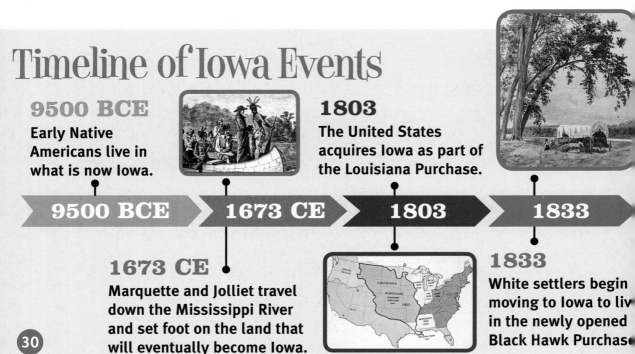

Timeline of Iowa Events

9500 BCE
Early Native Americans live in what is now Iowa.

1803
The United States acquires Iowa as part of the Louisiana Purchase.

9500 BCE → 1673 CE → 1803 → 1833

1673 CE
Marquette and Jolliet travel down the Mississippi River and set foot on the land that will eventually become Iowa.

1833
White settlers begin moving to Iowa to live in the newly opened Black Hawk Purchase

Farms and Families

The first farmers planted wheat, which they ground for their own use or shipped downriver to sell. Next they planted corn, which also grew well in the rich Iowa soil. Hog farms followed. The corn could be fed to the growing hogs, and then the animals themselves could be sold. Before too long, most of the original prairie was gone, and Iowa was covered with farms.

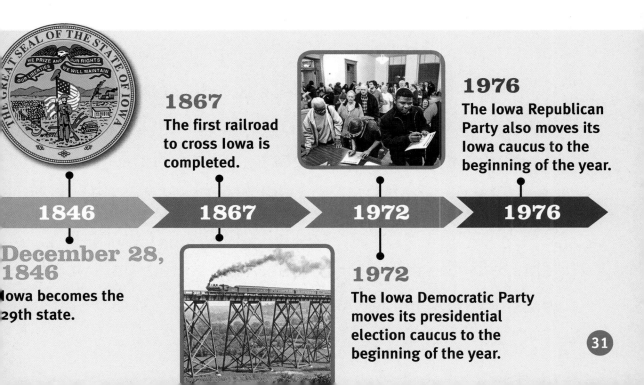

1867
The first railroad to cross Iowa is completed.

1976
The Iowa Republican Party also moves its Iowa caucus to the beginning of the year.

| 1846 | 1867 | 1972 | 1976 |

December 28, 1846
Iowa becomes the 29th state.

1972
The Iowa Democratic Party moves its presidential election caucus to the beginning of the year.

31

Today, there are more than 6,000 hog farms in Iowa.

Beginning in the 1860s, life changed for Iowans as railroads were built across the state. Farmers could now ship their products throughout the nation. Other industries also developed, including meatpacking plants and an oat-processing plant that eventually became part of the Quaker Oats company. Iowa prospered until the early 1900s, when the country entered World War I (1914–1918). After the war, many farmers had trouble paying their debts, and the following few decades were a time of hardship for many Iowa families.

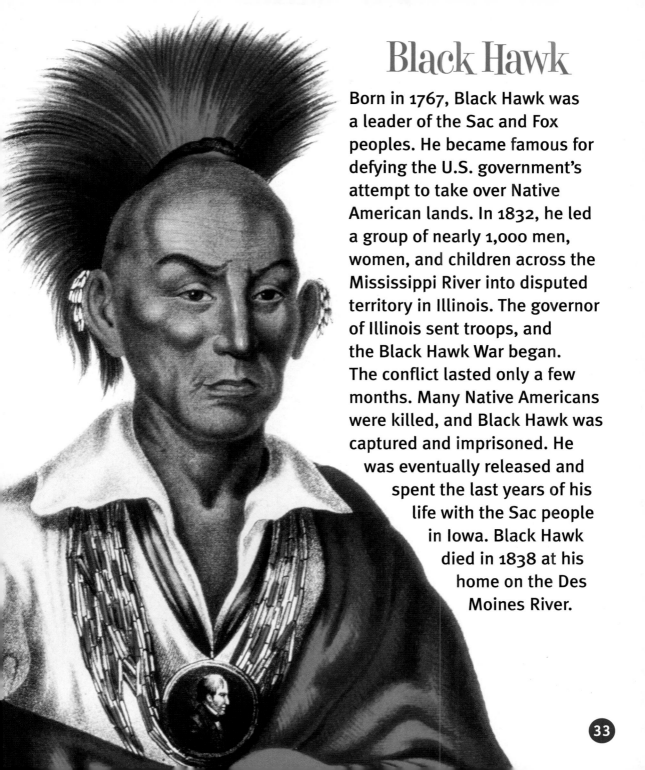

Black Hawk

Born in 1767, Black Hawk was a leader of the Sac and Fox peoples. He became famous for defying the U.S. government's attempt to take over Native American lands. In 1832, he led a group of nearly 1,000 men, women, and children across the Mississippi River into disputed territory in Illinois. The governor of Illinois sent troops, and the Black Hawk War began. The conflict lasted only a few months. Many Native Americans were killed, and Black Hawk was captured and imprisoned. He was eventually released and spent the last years of his life with the Sac people in Iowa. Black Hawk died in 1838 at his home on the Des Moines River.

Nearly 100 hot air-balloons take to the sky each summer at the National Balloon Classic in Indianola.

CHAPTER 4

Culture

There's more to Iowa than vast, rolling fields of corn. The state's oldest city, Dubuque, is home to the National Mississippi River Museum and Aquarium, where visitors can view river creatures and see a historical steamboat. The Cedar Rapids Museum of Art offers visitors the chance to see a great collection of paintings by American artist Grant Wood. Northwest of Des Moines are the Iowa Great Lakes, a string of lakes formed by glaciers that cover about 13,000 acres (5,261 ha).

Sports and Recreation

Iowa has no professional sports teams, but many Iowans are fans of college sports. The Iowa Hawkeyes are the athletic teams of the University of Iowa. The Iowa State Cyclones are based at Iowa State University. One of the biggest rivalries in the state is between the Hawkeyes and the Cyclones. Another famous sporting event is the Register's Annual Great Bicycle Ride Across Iowa (RAGBRAI), a cross-state bicycle ride held each summer.

RAGBRAI started as a challenge between two newspaper columnists, but it has turned into the largest and longest recreational bicycle touring event in the world.

Pella's annual Tulip Time festival features a parade, musical performances, and more.

Iowa Celebrations

Iowa has many residents of Scandinavian descent. Nordic Fest celebrates this heritage every summer in the city of Decorah. Settlers from Holland founded the town of Pella in 1847, and every year the town celebrates with the Tulip Time festival. Other yearly events in Iowa include the National Balloon Classic in Indianola, a weeklong festival of hot-air balloons, and the gigantic Iowa State Fair, which attracts over a million people to Des Moines each summer.

Iowans at Work

Many people think of Iowa as a farming state, but it is manufacturing that makes up the largest part of the state's economy. Food processing, machinery, and electrical equipment are important businesses. There are still many farms in Iowa, though. The state is a leader in producing hogs, corn, soybeans, eggs, and oats. Renewable energy has become very important, and Iowa leads the nation in producing power from wind turbines.

A Changing Economy

In the early years of the 20th century, Iowa's economy was booming as farmers supplied food to a growing nation. The Great Depression of the 1930s and another farm crisis in the 1980s hit farmers hard, and many had a difficult time keeping their farms going. Manufacturing and other businesses developed, and gave Iowans opportunities to work in areas other than agriculture. Many of these new jobs were in cities, and, as a result, people began to move away from their family farms. The move away from farms has continued, and today about two-thirds of the state's residents live in urban areas.

Cities such as Des Moines offer a wider variety of jobs and services than Iowa's more rural areas.

Iowa's Famous Foods

It should come as no surprise that foods from the farm, such as pork chops, ham, and corn on the cob, are popular in Iowa. Morels, a type of wild mushroom, are also one of the signature foods of the state. Scotcharoos and "puppy chow" are two yummy desserts that are well known in Iowa.

 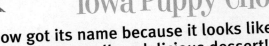 **Iowa Puppy Chow**

 Ask an adult to help you!

Puppy chow got its name because it looks like dry dog food, but it's actually a delicious dessert!

Ingredients
9 cups Rice Chex or Corn Chex cereal
1 cup semisweet chocolate chips
$1/2$ cup smooth peanut butter

$1/4$ cup butter or margarine
1 teaspoon vanilla extract
$1 1/2$ cups powdered sugar

Directions
Place the cereal in a large bowl. Combine the chocolate chips, peanut butter, butter or margarine, and vanilla in a microwave-safe bowl. Microwave for 30 seconds and stir. Microwave for another 20 seconds. Repeat until the mixture is smooth and creamy. Pour over the cereal and stir until the cereal is coated with the mixture. Place the sugar in a large ziplock bag. Add the cereal and shake until it is covered with the sugar. Spread onto waxed paper. Let cool completely, then store in an airtight container.

Children cool off under a sprinkler on a hot summer day in Davenport.

An Amazing Place to Be

Iowa is famous for its farms, but there's so much more to discover in this midwestern state. From its prairie origins, Iowa has grown into a state that's known not just for farming, but also for manufacturing, renewable energy, and business. Iowa has museums, art, exciting sports, all kinds of festivals, great food, and beautiful scenery. In short, Iowa offers something for everyone! ★

Famous People

George Washington Carver

(ca. 1864–1943) was a scientist and inventor who developed many important farming techniques. He attended Iowa State University and later taught there as well.

William Frederick "Buffalo Bill" Cody

(1846–1917) was a bison hunter, gold prospector, and showman. He was famous as one of the most colorful characters of the Old West. He was born in Le Claire.

Mamie Eisenhower

(1896–1979) was First Lady of the United States for eight years when her husband, Dwight D. Eisenhower, was president from 1953 to 1961. She was born in Boone.

Herbert Hoover

(1874–1964) was the 31st president of the United States. He was born in West Branch.

Glenn Miller

(1904–1944) was a noted orchestra leader and trombone player. He was born in Clarinda.

John Wayne

(1907–1979) was an actor who starred in 142 films. Nicknamed "Duke," he is best known for playing cowboys, cavalrymen, and other figures from the American West. He was a native of Winterset.

Ann Landers

(1918–2002) published a newspaper advice column for 47 years, reaching some 90 million readers. Her real name was Eppie Lederer, and she was from Sioux City.

Johnny Carson

(1925–2005) was a talk show host and comedian. He is best known for his 30 years as host of *The Tonight Show*. He was born in Corning.

Herbie Hancock

(1940–) is a Grammy award–winning keyboardist and composer who is considered one of the greatest jazz musicians in history. He earned multiple degrees while studying at Iowa's Grinnell College.

Janet Guthrie

(1938–) is a retired race car driver who was the first woman to race in the Indianapolis 500 and the Daytona 500. She is from Iowa City.

Peggy Whitson

(1960–) is a NASA biochemist and astronaut who holds records for the most time spent in space by any American (665 days) and the most spacewalks of any woman astronaut (10 spacewalks). She grew up near Beaconsfield.

Lara Flynn Boyle

(1970–) is an actor who is well known for her work in films such as *Wayne's World* and *Men in Black II*, as well as many television shows. She was born in Davenport.

Did You Know That...

Nearly one-third of the nation's hogs are raised in Iowa. There are seven times as many pigs as people in the state.

The Quaker Oats plant in Cedar Rapids is the largest cereal production plant in the world.

Iowa's biggest export is corn, and its second-biggest export is tractors.

Iowa's hens lay nearly 15 billion eggs each year!

Iowa produces a higher percentage of its electricity using wind than any other state.

Iowa is the only state in the United States whose eastern and western borders are formed entirely by rivers.

Did you find the truth?

T Much of Iowa's tallgrass prairie has been destroyed and replaced by farmland.

F Iowa is one of our nation's most densely populated states.

Resources

Books

Blashfield, Jean F. *Iowa*. New York: Children's Press, 2015.

Marciniak, Kristin. *What's Great About Iowa?* Minneapolis: Lerner Publications, 2015.

Rau, Dana Meachen. *The Midwest*. New York: Children's Press, 2012.

Rozett, Louise (ed.). *Fast Facts About the 50 States: Plus Puerto Rico and Washington, D.C.* New York: Children's Press, 2010.

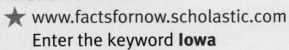

Visit this Scholastic website for more information on Iowa:

★ www.factsfornow.scholastic.com
Enter the keyword **Iowa**

Important Words

agriculture (AG-ri-kuhl-chur) the raising of crops and animals

caucus (KAW-kuhs) a closed meeting of members of a political party or faction usually to select candidates or decide policy

climate (KLYE-mit) the weather typical of a place over a long period of time

colonies (KAH-luh-neez) territories that have been settled by people from another country

ecosystem (EE-koh-sis-tuhm) all the living things in a place and their relationship to their environment

elevation (el-uh-VAY-shuhn) the height above sea level

glaciers (GLAY-shurz) slow-moving masses of ice found in mountain valleys or polar regions

habitats (HAB-ih-tats) the places where an animal or plant is usually found

prairie (PRAIR-ee) large area of flat or rolling grassland with few or no trees

terrain (tuh-RAYN) an area of land

territory (TER-i-tor-ee) an area connected with or owned by a country that is outside the country's main borders

Index

Page numbers in **bold** indicate illustrations.

About the Author

Ann O. Squire is a psychologist and an animal behaviorist. Before becoming a writer, she studied the behavior of rats, tropical fish in the Caribbean, and electric fish from central Africa. Her favorite part of being a writer is the chance to learn as much as she can about all sorts of topics. In addition to Iowa, Dr. Squire has written books about many types of animals, as well as health, earth science, planets, and weather. She lives in Asheville, North Carolina.